HERE, BULLET

Brian Turner served for seven years in the US Army. He was an infantry team leader for a year in Iraq from November 2003 with the 3rd Stryker Brigade Combat Team, 2nd Infantry Division. In 1999-2000 he was deployed to Bosnia-Herzegovina with the 10th Mountain Division. Born in 1967, he received an MFA from the University of Oregon and lived abroad in South Korea for a year before joining the army.

His poetry was included in the *Voices in Wartime Anthology* published in conjunction with a feature-length documentary film. His collection *Here, Bullet* (Bloodaxe Books, 2007) was first published by Alice James Books in the US in 2005, where it has earned Turner nine major literary awards, including a 2006 Lannan Literary Fellowship and a 2007 NEA Literature Fellowship in Poetry. In 2009 he was given an Amy Lowell Traveling Fellowship. Published in 2010 by Alice James Books in the US and by Bloodaxe Books in the UK, his second collection, *Phantom Noise* was shortlisted for the 2010 T.S. Eliot Prize.

BRIAN TURNER

HERE,
BULLET

BLOODAXE BOOKS

ISBN: 978 1 85224 799 7

This edition first published 2007 by
Bloodaxe Books Ltd,
Highgreen,
Tarset,
Northumberland NE48 1RP.

Second impression 2011.

Original US edition first published 2005
by Alice James Books, Farmington, Maine
www.alicejamesbooks.org

www.bloodaxebooks.com
For further information about Bloodaxe titles
please visit our website or write to
the above address for a catalogue.

Supported by
**ARTS COUNCIL
ENGLAND**

Cover design: Neil Astley & Pamela Robertson-Pearce.

Printed in Great Britain by
Bell & Bain Limited, Glasgow, Scotland.

CONTENTS

IV

ACKNOWLEDGEMENTS

Here, Bullet was first published in the US in 2005 by Alice James Books. This first UK edition reprints the contents of that book, with the addition of two poems not included in the original American edition, 'Notes from an Iranian Prisoner of War Camp' and 'The Martyrs Brigade'.

Grateful acknowledgement is made to the following publications in which these poems appeared, sometimes in slightly different forms: *The Cimarron Review*: 'Eulogy' and '16 Iraqi Policemen'; *Crab Orchard Review*: 'Ashbah', 'The Hurt Locker', 'Katyusha Rockets', 'To Sand' and 'Caravan'; *The Georgia Review*, Fall 2004: 'Gilgamesh, In Fossil Relief', 'Body Bags' and 'Here, Bullet'; *The Georgia Review*, Fall 2005: 'Hwy 1', 'The Al Harishma Weapons Market', 'Observation Post #71', 'Two Stories Down', 'Autopsy', 'Ferris Wheel', 'Dreams from the Malaria Pills (Barefoot)', 'Cole's Guitar', 'Tigris River Blues' and '9-Line Medevac'; *Magma*: 'Alhazen of Basra'; *The Massachusetts Review*: 'In the Leupold Scope' and 'From the Malaria Pills (Bosch)'; Natural Bridge: '2000 lbs', '*Milh*', and 'The Baghdad Zoo'.

In addition, '2000 lbs.', 'A Soldier's Arabic' and 'Sadiq' were included in the *Voices in Wartime Anthology*. 'Here, Bullet' was featured on *Poetry Daily* (www.poems.org) on November 8, 2004. And *From the Fishouse* (www.fishousepoems. org) features audio and text of 'Caravan', 'The Hurt Locker', 'Eulogy', 'Body Bags', 'Last Night's Dream', 'Here, Bullet', 'Gilgamesh, in Fossil Relief' and 'A Soldier's Arabic'.

For lyrics from 'Black Wind Blowing': words by Woody Guthrie, copyright © 2000 by Woody Guthrie Publications, Inc. All rights reserved, used by permission.

My deepest gratitude to the following: Aliki Barnstone, Tony Barnstone, Jeff Bell, Lane Chisholm, J. Glenn Evans, Anca Gabriela, Patsy Garoupa, Corrinne Clegg Hales, Karen Havenaer, Garret Hongo, Joe and Suzie Jantzen, Ave Jeanne, Dorianne Laux, Philip Levine, Michael Magee, Adrian Matejka, Clay Matthews, Joe Millar, Jeanne Musser, Matt O'Donnell, Michael Sauerwein, Joseph Sharpe, Evan Smith, Tad Benoit Band of New Orleans, Daniel Veach, Connie Walle, and Ellen Doré Watson. I wish to express special thanks for support given to me by my family, Brian Voight and Stacey Lynn Brown.

To Fi, Jax, Bosch, Z, Liu, Noodles, Knight, Hath, Zoo, Whitt, Bodiggidy, Shaft, Hardgrove, Nurse Betty, V, Klessig, R. Southerland, and our Iraqi translators (Harith, Jargis, Koder, Louie, and Saier) – *thank you*.

A Soldier's Arabic

*This is a strange new kind of war where you learn
just as much as you are able to believe.*
ERNEST HEMINGWAY

The word for love, *habib*, is written from right
to left, starting where we would end it
and ending where we might begin.

Where we would end a war
another might take as a beginning,
or as an echo of history, recited again.

Speak the word for death, *maut*,
and you will hear the cursives of the wind
driven into the veil of the unknown.

This is a language made of blood.
It is made of sand, and time.
To be spoken, it must be earned.

I

Who brings forth the living from the dead,
and the dead from the living?

The Baghdad Zoo

Is the world safer? No. It's not safer in Iraq.
HANS BLIX

An Iraqi northern brown bear mauled a man
on a street corner, dragging him down an alley
as shocked onlookers shouted and threw stones.

Tanks rolled their heavy tracks
past the museum and up to the Ministry of Oil.
A gunner watched a lion chase down a horse.

Eaten down to their skeletons, the giraffes
looked prehistoric, unreal, their necks
too fragile, too graceful for the 21st Century.

Dalmatian pelicans and marbled teals
flew over, frightened by the rotorwash
of Blackhawk helicopters touching down.

One baboon escaped the city limits.
It was found wandering in the desert, confused
by the wind, the blowing sands of the barchan dunes.

Hwy 1

I see a horizon lit with blood,
And many a starless night.
A generation comes and another goes
And the fire keeps burning.

AL-JAWAHIRI

It begins with the Highway of Death,
with an untold number of ghosts
wandering the road at night, searching
for the way home, to Najaf, Kirkuk,
Mosul and Kanni al Saad. It begins here
with a shuffling of feet on the long road north.

This is the spice road of old, the caravan trail
of camel dust and heat, where Egyptian limes
and sultani lemons swayed in crates
strapped down by leather, where merchants
traded privet flowers and musk, aloes,
honeycombs and silk brought from the Orient.

Past Marsh Arabs and the Euphrates wheel,
past wild camels and waving children
who marvel at the painted guns, the convoy
pushes on, past the ruins of Babylon and Sumer,
through the land of Gilgamesh where the minarets
sound the muezzin's prayer, resonant and deep.

Cranes roost atop power lines in enormous
bowl-shaped nests of sticks and twigs,
and when a sergeant shoots one from the highway
it pauses, as if amazed that death has found it
here, at 7 A.M. on such a beautiful morning,
before pitching over the side and falling
in a slow unraveling of feathers and wings.

In the Leupold Scope

With a 40x60mm spotting scope
I traverse the Halabjah skyline,
scanning rooftops two thousand meters out
to find a woman in sparkling green, standing
among antennas and satellite dishes,
hanging laundry on an invisible line.

She is dressing the dead, clothing them
as they wait in silence, the pigeons circling
as fumestacks billow a noxious black smoke.
She is welcoming them back to the dry earth,
giving them dresses in tangerine and teal,
woven cotton shirts dyed blue.

She waits for them to lean forward
into the breeze, for the wind's breath
to return the bodies they once had,
women with breasts swollen by milk,
men with shepherd-thin bodies, children
running hard into the horizon's curving lens.

The Al-Harishma Weapons Market

At midnight, steel shutters
slide down tight. Feral cats slink
in the periphery of the streetlamp's
dim cone of light. Inside, like a musician
swaddling a silver-plated trumpet,
Akbar wraps an AK-47 in cloth.
Grease guns, pistols, RPGs –
he slides them all under the countertop.

Black marketeer or insurgent –
an American death puts food on the table,
more cash than most men earn in an entire year.
He won't let himself think of his childhood friends –
those who wear the blue uniforms
which bring death, dying from barrels
he may have oiled in his own hands.

Akbar stirs the chai,
then carries his sleeping four-year-old,
Habib, to bed under glow-in-the-dark
stars arranged on the ceiling. Late at night
when gunfire frightens them both,
Habib cries for his father, who tells him
It's just the drums, a new music,
and the tracery of lights in the sky
he retraces on the ceiling, showing the boy
how each bright star travels
from this dark place, to the other.

What Every Soldier Should Know

To yield to force is an act of necessity, not of will;
it is at best an act of prudence.

JEAN-JACQUES ROUSSEAU

If you hear gunfire on a Thursday afternoon,
it could be for a wedding, or it could be for you.

Always enter a home with your right foot;
the left is for cemeteries and unclean places.

O-guf! Tera armeek is rarely useful.
It means *Stop! Or I'll shoot.*

Sabah el khair is effective.
It means *Good Morning.*

Inshallah means *Allah be willing.*
Listen well when it is spoken.

You will hear the RPG coming for you.
Not so the roadside bomb.

There are bombs under the overpasses,
in trashpiles, in bricks, in cars.

There are shopping carts with clothes soaked
in foogas, a sticky gel of homemade napalm.

Parachute bombs and artillery shells
sewn into the carcasses of dead farm animals.

Graffiti sprayed onto the overpasses:
I will kell you, American.

Men wearing vests rigged with explosives
walk up, raise their arms and say *Inshallah.*

There are men who earn eighty dollars
to attack you, five thousand to kill.

Small children who will play with you,
old men with their talk, women who offer chai –

and any one of them
may dance over your body tomorrow.

The Hurt Locker

Nothing but hurt left here.
Nothing but bullets and pain
and the bled-out slumping
and all the *fucks* and *goddamns*
and *Jesus Christs* of the wounded.
Nothing left here but the hurt.

Believe it when you see it.
Believe it when a twelve-year-old
rolls a grenade into the room.
Or when a sniper punches a hole
deep into someone's skull.
Believe it when four men
step from a taxicab in Mosul
to shower the street in brass
and fire. Open the hurt locker
and see what there is of knives
and teeth. Open the hurt locker and learn
how rough men come hunting for souls.

Observation Post #71

Balad, Iraq

Owls rest in the vines of wild grapes.
Eucalyptus trees shimmer.
And from the minaret, a voice.

Each life has its moment. The sunflowers
lift their faces toward dawn
as milk cows bellow in a field of trash.

I have seen him in the shadows.
I have watched him in the circle of light
my rifle brings to me. His song
hums in the wings of sand flies.
My mind has become very clear.

Here, Bullet

If a body is what you want,
then here is bone and gristle and flesh.
Here is the clavicle-snapped wish,
the aorta's opened valves, the leap
thought makes at the synaptic gap.
Here is the adrenaline rush you crave,
that inexorable flight, that insane puncture
into heat and blood. And I dare you to finish
what you've started. Because here, Bullet,
here is where I complete the word you bring
hissing through the air, here is where I moan
the barrel's cold esophagus, triggering
my tongue's explosives for the rifling I have
inside of me, each twist of the round
spun deeper, because here, Bullet,
here is where the world ends, every time.

Body Bags

A murder of crows looks on in silence
from the eucalyptus trees above
as we stand over the bodies –
who look as if they might roll over,
wake from a dream and question us
about the blood drying on their scalps,
the bullets lodged in the back of their skulls,
to ask where their wives and children are
this morning, and why this hovering
of flies, the taste of flatbread and chai
gone from their mouths as they stretch
and rise, wondering who these strangers are
who would kick their hard feet, saying
Last call, motherfucker. Last call.

AB Negative (The Surgeon's Poem)

Thalia Fields lies under a gray ceiling of clouds,
just under the turbulence, with anesthetics
dripping from an IV into her arm,
and the flight surgeon says *The shrapnel*
cauterised as it traveled through her
here, breaking this rib as it entered,
burning a hole through the left lung
to finish in her back, and all of this
she doesn't hear, except perhaps as music –
that faraway music of people's voices
when they speak gently and with care,
a comfort to her on a stretcher
in a flying hospital en route to Landstahl,
just under the rain at midnight, and Thalia
drifts in and out of consciousness
as a nurse dabs her lips with a moist towel,
her palm on Thalia's forehead, her vitals
slipping some, as burned flesh gives way
to the heat of blood, the tunnels within
opening to fill her, just enough blood
to cough up and drown in; Thalia
sees shadows of people working
to save her, but cannot feel their hands,
cannot hear them any longer,
and when she closes her eyes
the most beautiful colors rise in darkness,
tangerine washing into Russian blue,
with the droning engine humming on
in a dragonfly's wings, island palms
painting the sky an impossible hue
with their thick brushes dripping green...
a way of dealing with the fact
that Thalia Fields is gone, long gone,
about as far from Mississippi
as she can get, ten thousand feet above Iraq
with a blanket draped over her body
and an exhausted surgeon in tears,
his bloodied hands on her chest, his head
sunk down, the nurse guiding him

to a nearby seat and holding him as he cries,
though no one hears it, because nothing can be heard
where pilots fly in blackout, the plane
like a shadow guiding the rain, here
in the droning engines of midnight.

Two Stories Down

When he jumped from the balcony, Hasan swam
in the air over the Ashur Street Market,
arms and legs suspended in a blur
above palm hearts and crates of lemons,
not realising just how hard life fights
sometimes, how an American soldier
would run to his aid there on the sidewalk,
trying to make sense of Hasan's broken legs,
his screaming, trying to comfort him
with words in an awkward music
of stress and care, a soldier he'd startle
by stealing the knife from its sheath,
the two of them struggling for the blade
until the bloodgroove sunk deep
and Hasan whispered to him,
Shukran, sadiq, shukran;
Thank you, friend, thank you.

Ashbah

The ghosts of American soldiers
wander the streets of Balad by night,

unsure of their way home, exhausted,
the desert wind blowing trash
down the narrow alleys as a voice

sounds from the minaret, a soulful call
reminding them how alone they are,

how lost. And the Iraqi dead,
they watch in silence from rooftops
as date palms line the shore in silhouette,

leaning toward Mecca when the dawn wind blows.

Into the Elephant Grass

on the outskirts of Mosul

She scrubs clothes by hand in gasoline,
in a metal bucket just outside the tent.
At dawn, she hangs the laundry,
sheep eat from opened bags of trash,
mangy dogs yawn and stretch their backs
and ducks wade in a rivulet
of green and brackish water.

By noon, the world is reduced to heat.
The flatbeds have sold their iceblocks
and streets have turned to dust.
What is there to do but carve fruit
with sharpened knives, holding tears back
when her daughter traces the branding ink
tattooed on her cheek, line by line.

When the moon rises over Mosul
and the dogs have laid their muzzles down
to sleep, she follows her own shadow
into the elephant grass, into that thin-bladed
wall of green swaying fifteen feet high,
moving until her feet reach the water's edge,
where she undresses, loosening her *hejab*
and laying it down, easing her body
out into the dark water, cooling her
better than she ever imagined it would.

Eulogy

It happens on a Monday, at 11:20 A.M.,
as tower guards eat sandwiches
and seagulls drift by on the Tigris River.
Prisoners tilt their heads to the west
though burlap sacks and duct tape blind them.
The sound reverberates down concertina coils
the way piano wire thrums when given slack.
And it happens like this, on a blue day of sun,
when Private Miller pulls the trigger
to take brass and fire into his mouth:
the sound lifts the birds up off the water,
a mongoose pauses under the orange trees,
and nothing can stop it now, no matter what
blur of motion surrounds him, no matter what voices
crackle over the radio in static confusion,
because if only for this moment the earth is stilled,
and Private Miller has found what low hush there is
down in the eucalyptus shade, there by the river.

PFC B. Miller
(1980 – March 22, 2004)

II

This is war, then: All is well.
The missiles bomb the cities, and the airplanes bid the clouds farewell.
It is nothing but a corpse which grows and stretches...
Between time and time,
Between blood and blood.
All is well.

FADHIL AL-AZZAWI

Kirkuk Oilfield, 1927

We live on the roof of Hell, he says,
and Ahmed believes it, he's watched the gas flares
rise from holes in the earth, he's seen the black river
wash through the village in a flood of oil
as if the drillers had struck a vein
deep in the skull of God, and the old man says
Boy, you must learn how to live here –
where the dead are buried deep in the mind
of God, manifest in man and woman,
given to earth in dark blood,
given to earth in fire.

Trowel

The day before the Kurdish holiday
Hussein and Abid stir the muddy paste
with a shovel and their bare hands.

Because Hussein's arm is scarred
elbow to wrist from the long war with Iran,
he holds the trowel in his left hand, pushing

mud against a bullet-pocked wall, the cement
an appeasement which Hussein pauses over,
waiting out his hand's familiar tremor,

then burying the lead, its signatures
like dirt-filled sockets of bone
which he smoothes over and over.

Where the Telemetries End

Such is life:
we make love and the dry sheets
crackle in blue sparks. Water
slides vein by vein
over the face of stone.
We share a long night
of breathing. And when the dead
speak to us, we must ask them
to wait, to be patient,
for the night is still ours
on the rooftops of Al Ma'badi,
with a tracery of lights
falling all around us.

Autopsy

Camp Wolverine, Kuwait

Staff Sergeant Garza, the mortuary affairs specialist
from Missouri, switches on the music to hear
there's a long black cloud hanging in the sky, honey,
as she slices out a Y-incision with a scalpel
from collarbone to breastplate, from the xiphoid process
down the smooth skin of the belly, bringing light
into the great cavern of the body, in the deep flesh
where she cuts the cords which bind the heart,
lifting it in her gloved palms, weighing
and measuring the organ, she can't help
but imagine how fast it beat when he first kissed
Shawna Allen, or how it became heavy
with whiskey and what humbled him.
What Garza holds in her hands,
thirty-four years of a life, will be given
in ash to the earth and sea
if we're lucky, by someone like her,
singing low at the chorus
there's a long black cloud hanging in the sky,
weather's gonna break and hell's gonna fly,
baby, sweet thing, darlin.

Repatriation Day

Shalamcheh, at the Iran-Iraq border

The skeletons rest in their boxes
still slack-jawed twenty years later,
as if amazed at their own deaths.

I want to lie down among them,
to be wrapped in sheets like the flags
of nations, banded in light and shadow.

I want the Red Cross worker to lean over,
so I can see that tired look in her eyes
as she writes down my name.

(for Koder)

Notes from an Iranian Prisoner of War Camp

for Louie, of Hamman al Alil

It is the winter of 1989, Tehran.
Louie stares over the prison walls
as ski-lifts rise on their high-tension wires
up the steep canyons, disappearing
into a deciduous canopy, dusted in snow.

To the north, Mount Damavand stands
highest among the Alborz mountains,
with black-bearded goats staring out
toward the Caspian Sea, their spiraling horns
strange as a dream to Louie, who wonders
if he'll ever see his mother's hands again
making flatbread on the oven outside,
if he'll ever hear his wife's soft breath
on the rooftops of Al Ma'badi, late at night
when the children have drifted off in sleep,
or if he'll see the Tigris again, rolling.

Tragedy is in the unfinished life.
Ask Louie. Sit beside him there
on the train from Tehran to the camps
in the North. Listen to him tell the story
of the Mil-e Gonbad Tower, which stands
just outside, there to the left, 180 feet high
and a thousand years old, built to last
forever by a prince, a poet, a scholar,
a man who understood the need for perspective.

Don't ask about freedom. Don't search
for pain in the stories he tells of walls,
and seasons. Don't imagine yourself understanding.
The lines in his face are his alone to bear.
Twelve years imprisoned for a war
long since finished, and still, when he speaks
of Tehran, he speaks of waterfalls and beauty,
he speaks of fog and snow on the mountainsides,
the bright wings of men coming down.

The Martyrs Brigade

I hide a disaster behind the mask of words; I say to my wound:
'Don't heal', and to my grief: 'Don't abate';
and to lovers I say: 'Wash in my blood.'

ABD AL-WAHHAB AL-BAYYATI

The poets eat kahi and drink cardamon tea
    in Baghdad, and it could be 1948
or 2004, it could be British bombers
    overhead, or the 173rd Airborne
parachuting down from a metal-blue sky,
    but these poets will soon be dead,
and bridges will be blown all over Iraq,
    verses I cannot even translate
will be lost forever, lost the way bodies
    carry their bullets to the grave,
their wounds closed only by the earth
    thrown over, shovel by shovel,
the burial of the 1920 Revolution Brigade
    to be repeated again in '48
with the Wathbah uprising, and again
    it must seem, with the fighters
in Tikrit, in Samarra, in Mosul and Fallouja,
    Jisr Al-Shuhada they cry,
for *The Martyrs Brigade* they would die,
    life is given purpose in struggle,
at least for the young, and the passionate,
    for those who discover in fire
an echo of the searing heat of their own veins,
    and if I could, I'd be there
on the bridge with Al-Jawahiri in 1948,
    with government bullets in the air,
my friend's brother dying in his arms even now,
    and I would hold back the blood
with my own hands, if only to be there
    and to ask them both before dying,
Is it worth it? Can there be no other way?

Najaf, 1820

Camel caravans transport the dead
from Persia and beyond, their bodies dried
and wrapped in carpets, their dying wishes
to be buried near Ali,
                    where the first camel
dragged Ali's body across the desert
tied to the fate of its exhaustion.
Najaf is where the dead naturally go,
where the gates of Paradise open before them
in unbanded light, the blood washed clean
from their bodies.
                    It is November,
the clouds made of gunpowder and rain,
the earth pregnant with the dead;
cemetery mounds stretching row by row
with room enough yet for what the years
will bring: the gravediggers need only dig,
shovel by shovel.

For Vultures: A Dystopia

For their hunger, for their patience,
for each circle traced in shadow
and sunk down in the earth
I offer the remorse of flesh,
unflowered and darkening, my life
a gift of heat and steam.

Today, the sun is as high
as the arc of the heavens
will carry it. Let the vultures rise, too.
Let them witness every plume
of smoke, every fallen soldier,
every woman's last kiss
for the ones they love,
and even me when the time comes,
let the vultures feed on me,
let them tear me apart.

16 Iraqi Policemen

The explosion left a hole in the roadbed
large enough to fit a mid-sized car.
It shattered concrete, twisted metal,
busted storefront windows in sheets
and lifted a BMW chassis up onto a rooftop.

The shocking blood of the men
forms an obscene art: a moustache, alone
on a sidewalk, a blistered hand's gold ring
still shining, while a medic, Doc Lopez,
pauses to catch his breath, to blow it out
hard, so he might cup the left side of a girl's face
in one hand, gently, before bandaging
the half gone missing.

Allah must wander in the crowd
as I do, dazed by the pure concussion
of the blast, among sirens, voices
of the injured, the boots of running soldiers,
not knowing whom to touch first,
for the dead policemen cannot be found,
here a moment before, then vanished.

Dreams from the Malaria Pills (Barefoot)

Tamaghis ba'dan yaswadda waghdas nawfana ghadis

He's coughing up shrapnel, jagged and rough,
wondering if this is what the incantation brings,
those dreamwords shaping desire into being.

He's questioning why blood is needed, and so much,
why he's wheeled through his hometown streets
on a gurney draped in camouflaged sheets.

Ibn Khaldun takes each piece of metal from him:
These are to be made into daggers,
precious gifts, the souvenirs of death.

You carry the pearls of war within you, bombs
swallowed whole and saved for later.
Give them to your children. Give them to your love.

Katyusha Rockets

The 107s have a crackling sound
of fire and electricity, of air-ruckled heat,
and when they pinwheel over the rooftops
of Hamman al Alil
                              they just keep going,
traveling for years over the horizon
to land in the meridians of Divisadero Street,
where I'm standing early one morning
on a Memorial Day in Fresno, California,
the veteran's parade scattering at the impact,
mothers shielding their children by instinct,
old war vets crouching behind automobiles
as police set up an outer cordon
for the unexploded ordinance.
                              Rockets often fall
in the night sky of the skull, down long avenues
of the brain's myelin sheathing, over synapses
and the rough structures of thought, they fall
into the hippocampus, into the seat of memory –
where lovers and strangers and old friends
entertain themselves, unaware of the dangers
headed their way, or that I will need to search
among them
                    the way the bomb disposal tech
walks tethered and alone down Divisadero Street,
suited-up as if walking on the moon's surface
as the crowd watches just how determined he is
to dismantle death, to take it apart
piece by piece – the bravest thing I've ever seen.

R&R

The curve of her hip where I'd lay my head,
that's what I'm thinking of now, her fingers
gone slow through my hair on a blue day
ten thousand miles off in the future somewhere,
where the beer is so cold it sweats in your hand,
cool as her kissing you with crushed ice,
her tongue wet with blackberry and melon.

That's what I'm thinking of now.
Because I'm all out of adrenaline,
all out of smoking incendiaries.

Somewhere deep in the landscape of the brain,
under the skull's blue curving dome –
that's where I am now, swaying
in a hammock by the water's edge
as soldiers laugh and play volleyball
just down the beach, while others tan
and talk with the nurses who bring pills
to help them sleep. And if this is crazy,
then let this be my sanatorium,
let the doctors walk among us here
marking their charts as they will.

I have a lover with hair that falls
like autumn leaves on my skin.
Water that rolls in smooth and cool
as anesthesia. Birds that carry
all my bullets into the barrel of the sun.

Dreams from the Malaria Pills (Bosch)

Forward Operating Base Anaconda, Iraq

This time, it's 5 A.M. Lucid.
Bosch can see his own hands
lifting water to his face.
Sees himself reflected in the mirror,
an image of infinity, shaving
his beard and neck, the blade
silver and sharp under fluorescent light,
as he reaches back with the razor
to scrape it over the smooth dome
of consciousness, that concentric heat
peeling in strips like a rind of fruit,
the skin of a peach, down the forehead
and over eyebrows, cheek, and jaw,
sloughing the blood and skin in sinkwater,
repeating this, over and over again,
his eyes focused, unfazed.

❧

Tonight, he lies in his bunk. The smoky moon
cools its muzzle of light with a cloudy trail.
Bosch soaks his forearms in lighter-fluid,
flares a match head and sets his skin on fire.
He repeats this to his thighs and calves.
He burns his chest like a savanna.
By morning, even his head is on fire
as the sun rises up over the earth at dawn
like the opened mouth of a flamethrower, 140 degrees.

How Bright It Is

April. And the air dry
as the shoulders of a water buffalo.

Grasshoppers scratch at the dirt,
rub their wings with thin legs,
flaring out in front of the soldiers
in low arcing flights, wings a blur.

The soldiers don't notice anymore,
seeing only the wreckage of the streets,
bodies draped with sheets, and the sun,
how bright it is, how hard and flat and white.

It will take many nails from the coffinmakers
to shut out this light, which reflects off everything:
the calloused feet of the dead, their bony hands,
their pale foreheads so cold, brilliant in the sun.

III

Do they not see the birds above their heads,
spreading their wings and closing them?

QUR'AN 67:19

Alhazen of Basra

If I could travel a thousand years back
to August 1004, to a small tent
where Alhazen has fallen asleep among books
about sunsets, shadows, and light itself,
I wouldn't ask whether light travels in a straight line,
or what governs the laws of refraction, or how
he discovered the bridgework of analytical geometry;
I would ask about the light within us,
what shines in the mind's great repository
of dream, and whether he's studied the deep shadows
daylight brings, how light defines us.

Easel

Nathere loads the brush with river-blue oil,
mixes it with yellow cadmium and stone
to paint a sky made of light and dust,
where ravens fly and date palms open
in a burst of green, with no trunks
painted in to hold them, the shiny fronds
drifting like epiphytes on the wind.

Nathere pauses, unsure.
There is too much heat. Figures of people
fade into a canvas blur, mere phantasms
of paint, their features unrecoverable, their legs
disappearing beneath them as Nathere realises –
there are no shadows to hold them down,
no slant and fall of shadow,
light's counterpoint, the dark processing
of thought. All burns in light here,
all rises in heat as colored tongues
lift in flame, brushstroke by brushstroke,
an erasure the sky washes out in blue.

Observation Post #798

It is in the watches of the night
that impressions are strongest
and words most eloquent.

QUR'AN 73:1

Tonight, we overwatch the Market District
by the ruins, where we know of a brothel-house:
green light above the door, windows shuttered
in French panels swung open, gauze curtains
hanging translucent in the heat.

It's over a hundred degrees, even at dusk.
I scan each story with binoculars
and a smile, hoping to glimpse the girls
drawing open the curtains,
their silhouettes edged in light.

When a woman walks out onto the rooftop
smoking a cigarette and shaking loose her long hair,
everyone wants what I hold in my hands,
but I am stilled by her, transported 7,600 miles
away, as a ghost might gaze upon the one he loves,

thinking, *how lovely you are*,
your pain and beauty a fiction
I bend into the form of a bridge, anything
to remind me I am still alive.

2000 lbs

Ashur Square, Mosul

It begins simply with a fist, white-knuckled
and tight, glossy with sweat. With two eyes
in a rearview mirror watching for a convoy.
The radio a soundtrack that adrenaline has
pushed into silence, replacing it with a heartbeat,
his thumb trembling over the button.

&

A flight of gold, that's what Sefwan thinks
as he lights a Miami, draws in the smoke
and waits in his taxi at the traffic circle.
He thinks of summer 1974, lifting
pitchforks of grain high in the air,
the slow drift of it like the fall of Shatha's hair,
and although it was decades ago, he still loves her,
remembers her standing at the canebrake
where the buffalo cooled shoulder-deep in the water,
pleased with the orange cups of flowers he brought her,
and he regrets how so much can go wrong in a life,
how easily the years slip by, light as grain, bright
as the street's concussion of metal, shrapnel
traveling at the speed of sound to open him up
in blood and shock, a man whose last thoughts
are of love and wreckage, with no one there
to whisper him gone.

&

Sgt Ledouix of the National Guard
speaks but cannot hear the words coming out,
and it's just as well his eardrums ruptured
because it lends the world a certain calm,
though the traffic circle is filled with people
running in panic, their legs a blur
like horses in a carousel, turning
and turning the way the tires spin
on the Humvee flipped to its side,

51

the gunner's hatch he was thrown from
a mystery to him now, a dark hole
in metal the color of sand, and if he could,
he would crawl back inside of it,
and though his fingertips scratch at the asphalt
he hasn't the strength to move:
shrapnel has torn into his ribcage
and he will bleed to death in minutes,
but he finds himself surrounded by a strange
beauty, the shine of light on the broken,
a woman's hand touching his face, tenderly
the way his wife might, amazed to find
a wedding ring on his crushed hand,
the bright gold sinking in flesh
going to bone.

¿▲

Rasheed passes the bridal shop
on a bicycle, with Sefa beside him,
and just before the air ruckles and breaks
he glimpses the sidewalk reflections
in the storefront glass, men and women
walking and talking, or not, an instant
of clarity, just before each of them shatters
under the detonation's wave,
as if even the idea of them were being
destroyed, stripped of form,
the blast tearing into the manikins
who stood as though husband and wife
a moment before, who cannot touch
one another, who cannot kiss,
who now lie together in glass and debris,
holding one another in their half-armed embrace,
calling this love, if this is all there will ever be.

¿▲

The civil affairs officer, Lt Jackson, stares
at his missing hands, which make
no sense to him, no sense at all, to wave
these absurd stumps held in the air

where just a moment before he'd blown bubbles
out the Humvee window, his left hand holding the bottle,
his right hand dipping the plastic ring in soap,
filling the air behind them with floating spheres
like the oxygen trails of deep ocean divers,
something for the children, something beautiful,
translucent globes with their iridescent skins
drifting on vehicle exhaust and the breeze
that might lift one day over the Zagros mountains,
that kind of hope, small globes which may have
astonished someone on the sidewalk
seven minutes before Lt Jackson blacks out
from blood loss and shock, with no one there to bandage
the wounds that would carry him home.

❧

Nearby, an old woman cradles her grandson,
whispering, rocking him on her knees
as though singing him to sleep, her hands
wet with their blood, her black dress
soaked in it as her legs give out
and she buckles with him to the ground.
If you'd asked her forty years earlier
if she could see herself an old woman
begging by the roadside for money, here,
with a bomb exploding at the market
among all these people, she'd have said
To have your heart broken one last time
before dying, to kiss a child given sight
of a life he could never live? It's impossible,
this isn't the way we die.

❧

And the man who triggered the button,
who may have invoked the Prophet's name,
or not – he is obliterated at the epicenter,
he is everywhere, he is of all things,
his touch is the air taken in, the blast
and the wave, the electricity of shock,
his is the sound the heart makes quick

53

in the panic's rush, the surge of blood
searching for light and color, that sound
the martyr cries filled with the word
his soul is made of, *Inshallah.*

≈

Still hanging in the air over Ashur Square,
the telephone line snapped in two, crackling
a strange incantation the dead hear
as they wander confused amongst one another,
learning each other's names, trying to comfort
the living in their grief, to console
those who cannot accept such random pain,
speaking *habib* softly, one to another there
in the rubble and debris, *habib*
over and over, that it might not be forgotten.

Dreams from the Malaria Pills (Turner)

Forward Operating Base Eagle, Iraq

This time it's beautiful.
He's in the kelp beds somewhere
off the California coast, floating
where green leaves touch the sun,
as if he's disentangled
from thought itself, as if the mind
has come this far, up from the depths
to release him to the crests and shallows
drifting wave by wave back to shore.

He knows there are bombs
washed up on the beach. There are limbs
of people he has never met. Bandages
soaked in blood and salt.
He knows the Qur'an and the Bible
have washed page by page to shore,
their bindings stripped loose, their ink
blurred into the sea.

And if people are crying there,
wading out in the surf to carry it all
back in, then he hasn't seen them yet.
The ocean sounds in the bones
of his skull, and the albatross fly
reconnaissance over the waves,
searching for a route home.

Curfew

The wrong is not in the religion;
The wrong is in us.

SAIER T.

At dusk, bats fly out by the hundreds.
Water snakes glide in the ponding basins
behind the rubbled palaces. The mosques
call their faithful in, welcoming
the moonlight as prayer.

Today, policemen sunbathed on traffic islands
and children helped their mothers
string clothes to the line, a slight breeze
filling them with heat.

There were no bombs, no panic in the streets.
Sgt Gutierrez didn't comfort an injured man
who cupped pieces of his friend's brain
in his hands; instead, today,
white birds rose from the Tigris.

IV

Give me one last drink from the Tigris,
If I could, I would drink the whole river.

ABDUL 'ALA' AL-MA'ARRI
(973–1057 A.D.)

Mihrab

They say the Garden of Eden blossomed here
long ago, and this is all that remains,
wind scorpions and dust, crow-like jays
cawing their raspy throats in memory
of a song, a ghost of beauty
lingering in the shadow's fall.

Let me lie here and dream of a better life.
Let what beauty there is be lifted up
and given to the greater world
as I listen to the mouths of termites
eating of the earth, their bodies
drumming a rhythm in the soil, undaunted
in their blindness, by the millions
raising a skylined architecture
the blood moon must recognise with light.
Let me stay here with these birds
and listen to their rough songs.

If I say the desert is an afterimage,
that birds serenade us, that the moon
is the heart of God shining in heaven,
that if there is a heaven it is
so deep within us we are overgrown,
that the day brings only a stripping of leaves
and by sundown we are exhausted,
then let it be, because if there is a definition
in the absence of light,
and if a ghost can wander amazed
through the days of its life, then it is me,
here in the Garden of Eden,
where it is impossible to let go
of what we love and what we've lost,
here, where the breath of God is our own.

Milh

Ankle-deep in the white-ochre saltflats
north of Babylon, women harvest salt
with buckets and bare hands,
in stands of water the color
of rust, or a blue dark as oil
come up from the earth, as if
they walk on the water's surface
ablaze with sunlight, dressed in black,
the color of crows, the color of shadows,
as if they would burst upward in flame
under the lightest, most austere touch,
still, they cup their palms and reach
down with the cracked skin of their hands
softened by water, to lift what is precious,
the gold-leafed dust of antiquity
which washes and sifts through their fingers
and is lost, every time, leaving only
this distillate of salt which the sun burns
into a mineral-bright ash of white
they carry in reverence to shore.

Gilgamesh, in Fossil Relief

for Sin-lege-unninni

In the month of Ab, late summer
of the seventh century B.C.E., a poet
chisels text into stone tablets, etching
three thousand lines and brushing them by hand,
the dust blown off with a whispered breath.

He is translating the old Sumerian epic,
reinventing the city of Uruk, the Wild Man
and the woman sent out to seduce him.
It is an old story now. It was an old story then,
full of gods and beasts and the inevitable
points of no return each age must learn.

In the mid-August heat of the year 2004,
an archaeologist pauses over an outline
of bone, one body's signature in the earth,
which he reads carefully with a camelhair brush
and patience, each hairline fracture revealing.

History is a cloudy mirror made of dirt
and bone and ruin. And love? Loss?
These are the questions we must answer
by war and famine and pestilence, and again
by touch and kiss, because each age must learn
This is the path of the sun's journey by night.

Tigris River Blues

on Ambush Alley

There's a blood moon hung over the river.
A medevac request crosses the radio
in static, the details of a guntruck
sliding down a bank and into the fast dark waters
of summer, two men who didn't make it.

I've had too much bad sleep. Not enough coffee.
And the hours pass the way helicopters
hover above the palm groves
or the way Fiorillo reads letters from his wife
with a red lens flashlight, down in the troop hold.

There's a feeling I can't quite shake.
Everything has sunken into the abstruse.
I read my own red pages
as death whispers from the rotors.

The Tigris keeps its deep currents secret.
And tonight, as we drive for the lights of Balad,
the world glows night vision green
set against a sky of uncountable stars.

Ferris Wheel

Al Sadeer Tourist Complex, Mosul, Iraq

A helicopter went down in the river
last night, hitting a power line slung
a few feet off the water. They were searching
for survivors and bodies from a boat
capsized earlier, Americans and Iraqis both.

It's dawn now, and the sky
drifts low and flat and cold
the way search-boats on the Tigris
drift further and further downriver.
When Navy divers bring up the body
of an Iraqi policeman, it will be a man
we aren't searching for, and still another
later in the day – a college student from Kirkuk.

It will be a long week of searching
like this, every morning near the shoreline
restaurant, where open fires are fed
kindling and tinder, a cook's hands
lifting the silver bodies of fish,
weighing them on scales.

The history books will get it wrong.
There will be nothing written
about the island ferris wheel
frozen by rust like a broken clock, or
about the pilot floating unconscious downriver, sparks
fading above as his friend swam toward him
instead of the shore, how both would drown
in this cold unstoppable river.

Sadiq

It should make you shake and sweat,
nightmare you, strand you in a desert
of irrevocable desolation, the consequences
seared into the vein, no matter what adrenaline
feeds the muscle its courage, no matter
what god shines down on you, no matter
what crackling pain and anger
you carry in your fists, my friend,
it should break your heart to kill.

Jameel

Cowbirds rest in the groves of date palms,
whole flocks of them, white as flowers
blossoming into wings when the wind rises up.

Thistleweed bursts open in purple
while honeybees drone and hover
over the yellowing, early-summer field.

They say to produce one pound of honey,
bees must travel from flower to hive
at least twelve thousand times.

Such patience, waiting for this storm
to be carried over the far mountains,
when the earth darkens and the sky lowers

and cowbirds shield themselves under a wing,
the nectar swaying heavy within the closed flower,
the hive humming its prayer under the rain's falling hush.

Last Night's Dream

for Ishtar

In the dream her breasts become confused in my lips. I shoot an azimuth to her navel while her fingertips touch me with concussions, as if explosives rang through the nerves of my body, as if I am strung with wire, a huge receiver of UHF radio transmissions, frequency hopping with our tongues as we kiss and I slide into her with a sound of flashbang grenades that make her eyes cloud over in smoke from the heat of it.

In the dream she kisses Arabic into my skin and I understand every word of it, I transcribe it backwards into cuneiform and stone, I rename the arteries and veins for every river and wadi from Dohuk north to Basra south, I feel for this geography of pleasure, my tongue is a marker that writes even in the rain, even in salt and sweat, and I write with it now, over every curve and turn of her body.

In the dream our orgasm destroys a nation, it leaves thermite and gunpowder in the air above us, a crackling of radio static as we kiss on, long into the denouement of skin and fire, where medevac helicopters fly in the dark caverns of our lungs in search of the wounded, and we breathe them one to another, a deep rotorwash of pain and bandages.

Cole's Guitar

Al Ma'badi, Iraq

It's the sound from the aid station
that wakes me, thin steel
from Doc Cole's six-string,
a 4 A.M. sound of sour whiskey,
heroin and sex and dying,
that's the sound I'm hearing now,
slow as smoke from a factory
in Pittsburgh, slow as a needle
in the vein, slow as steam off the bath
or a lover with only the blues to sing.

I'm hearing America now.
I'm hearing jake brakes off the Grapevine,
county highways with wheat shocks
and Indian summergrass whispering,
foghorns under the Golden Gate bridge,
Ella Fitzgerald from a 4th floor window
in Birmingham, the handles of a suitcase
swinging on the downbeat of a man's footsteps
walking out from a Greyhound in Santa Fe.

I'm in Wyoming. I'm in New York.
I'm leaning in to kiss a woman
in the cornfields down by the river.
I'm with children drawing portraits
in the sand, old men watching fireflies
the way Muhammad Ali lay on the canvas
and dreamed. That's what I'm hearing,
the wind on the redwood coast,
old as the ocean and hushed
by sheets of fallen snow.

Palm-mute the strings, Doc,
strum that song until I can see
the breath on a bus window, the faces
of strangers in the rain, my own hands
tracing the features of every one of them,
the way ghosts might visit the ones they love,
as I am now, listening to America,
touching the cold glass.

9-Line Medevac

Medevac Line 1: Location of the pick-up site?

Any Sheriff in Baghdad, any Sheriff in Baghdad I say into the radio handmic, my hands shaking with adrenaline and stress and dehydration. I give a ten-digit grid for this exact spot on the earth's surface, the west side of Baghdad, the Highway 1 interchange we've renamed Route Victor, fifty meters north of the overpass, on the shoulder there, that's where they are, there in the dirt and wreckage, surrounded by tiered buildings with balconies crowded by the curious onlookers tragedy always lures in, and I can name this spot, but cannot make it real, cannot give it the crackling stress of the air here, how heavy and charged it is, or the smell of trashfires drifting noxious and sweet, or the position of the gibbous moon overhead, too eager for night as the sun is still slowed by the horizon at dusk, too eager to romanticise the land and maybe even what's happening, though there's nothing romantic about this, unless pain and sweat and heat and blood and a grown man pissing in his pants with fear are romantic, all of this and more is where we are, the clock stopped here, the day as yet unfinished, blood smeared on my forehead –

Medevac Line 2: Radio frequency – Call sign – Requesting unit?

I tell him the frequency though I am hearing everyone around the site now, sergeants yelling for *Stretchers, goddammit, I said get a goddamned stretcher and a spine board now*, and each voice is edged with that urgent pulse of the larynx, the vocal cords roughened by the lungs, I tell the Sheriff my call-sign is Ghost 1-3 Alpha, which is like telling him he speaks with the dead, and that the dead wish for his help, that the dead wait for him in Baghdad on asphalt stretched out flat as a river of oil, fuming –

Medevac Line 3: Number of patients by precedence?

I tell him *Two, two patients urgent surgical*, though that doesn't really tell him Sgt Randolph has four children and can't die here, his wife wouldn't allow it if she knew, and if she knew the shock of it snapped back his head and threw him down into the vehicle's troop compartment, if she knew that she'd fall to her knees, her ears would shut out the noise of the world to complete silence, that's how urgent this is, the Sheriff of Baghdad doesn't know Specialist Mundy has a chunk of shrapnel in his neck, just under the skin, and he's bleeding horribly, his eyes gone from black to a washed-out gray, the purple heart they will both be given for this is an award no one wants –

Medevac Line 4: At least give me line 4 so I can get the bird in the air, alright Soldier? Special equipment required?

Special equipment? Hoists? Ventilators? How do I know what will save them? Blood. Bring them blood, especially for Mundy, because that's more blood than I've ever seen before, spilled all over the vehicle seats and the ramp, my shirt, my hands, wiped onto my scalp, so much blood but I don't know what type, and send the best surgeon there is, someone who knows more than the mechanics of the body, someone who knows how to treat that drifting of the mind into the fizzling lights, how the mind seems to vanish into the skull's stratosphere of bone, untethered, rising to where the world ends, that edge, bring a doctor who can bring them back from there, and quick –

Medevac Line 5: Number of patients, by type?

Which makes me pause knowing they cannot walk and are litter patients, but the pause is a greater concern – to classify them forces me to admit I do not know these men I've worked beside, one I know has a bronze star for going into a mine field, and the other I know only as being a shy and quiet one, maybe twenty –

Medevac Line 6: Security?

Look around. No one knows who the enemy is. All of it looks like Thursday evening on a freeway cutting through town, wedding parties passing by firing AK-47s into the air, everything is possible here, everything...

Medevac Line 7: Method of marking the site?

The Sheriff of Baghdad needs to know – A smoke signal? An orange panel? How best do you mark a place of loss and pain? This is hallowed earth, and if one of them should die here – Flowers?

Stones? Will it have mourners dressed in black to stand by the roadside as boots and rifles are buried under the roadbed? Will it have angels to watch over the soul of Mundy, who believes in them?

Medevac Line 8: Patient's nationality?

If they die here, what will it matter? The plains of the Euphrates and Tigris Rivers, this land of confluence and heat will become their nation, and even if they live, it will be theirs as well – the land that tested their souls and changed them –

Medevac Line 9: Son, tell me the terrain, that's all we need and we'll be there for you

The land is what I need, soil ground into the heels of my palms, canebrakes in the canals, water buffalo up to their shoulders in dark water, the wind that brings the dust so thick it pales the sun dim as a daylight moon, this land, flat and hard, where sunflower fields grow thick with yellow heads hung down as if in respect for the losses being given and received, here where the Blackhawk flares down in a cloud of dust in the rotorwash I run into with Sgt Randolph's stretcher, a soldier who will never be the same.

Night in Blue

At seven thousand feet and looking back, running lights
blacked out under the wings and America waiting,
a year of my life disappears at midnight,
the sky a deep viridian, the houselights below
small as match heads burned down to embers.

Has this year made me a better lover?
Will I understand something of hardship,
of loss, will a lover sense this
in my kiss or touch? What do I know
of redemption or sacrifice, what will I have
to say of the dead – that it was worth it,
that any of it made sense?
I have no words to speak of war.
I never dug the graves in Talafar.
I never held the mother crying in Ramadi.
I never lifted my friend's body
when they carried him home.

I have only the shadows under the leaves
to take with me, the quiet of the desert,
the low fog of Balad, orange groves
with ice forming on the rinds of fruit.
I have a woman crying in my ear
late at night when the stars go dim,
moonlight and sand as a resonance
of the dust of bones, and nothing more.

Caravan

No matter the barking of the dogs,
the caravan marches on.

OLD IRAQI PROVERB

A long queue of container ships
stand at anchor in the Persian Gulf.
They carry .50 caliber machine guns
in packing grease, dunnage, ammo crates,
millions of bullets laid side by side,
toilet paper, insecticides, light bulbs.
The dockside floodlights hum
with mosquitoes and malaria. Cranes
hoist connexes onto flatbed trucks
which line Highway 1 from Kuwait City
to Dohuk in the north, just south of Turkey,
with enough boxes of food
for a hundred and thirty thousand meals,
two to three times a day for a year,
an army of commerce, a fleet
of corporations with the Pacific as its highway –
these are the boxes we bring to Iraq.
Today, in Baghdad, a bomb
kills forty-seven and wounds over one hundred,
leaving a crater ten feet deep. The stunned
gather body parts from the roadway
to collect in cardboard boxes
which will not be taped and shipped
to the White House lawn, not buried
under the green sod thrown over, box by box
emptied into the rich soil in silence
while a Marine sentry stands guard
at the National Monument, Tomb of the Unknown,
our own land given to these, to say
if this is freedom, then we will share it.

To Sand

To sand go tracers and ball ammunition.
To sand the green smoke goes.
Each finned mortar, spinning in light.
Each star cluster, bursting above.
To sand go the skeletons of war, year by year.
To sand go the reticles of the brain,
the minarets and steeple bells, brackish
sludge from the open sewers, trashfires,
the silent cowbirds resting
on the shoulders of a yak. To sand
each head of cabbage unravels its leaves
the way dreams burn in the oilfires of night.

NOTES

꿈

All the passages quoted from the Qur'an are from translator N.J. Dawood's *The Koran* (Penguin Books, 1974).

A Soldier's Arabic (11)
The epigraph is from Ernest Hemingway, 'War is Reflected Vividly in Madrid' (*New York Times*, 25 April 1937, p. 28).

Except where otherwise noted, all Arabic transliterations are from an Arabic-English/English-Arabic phrase book given to me by an Iraqi soldier. From the damaged cover I've ascertained it was edited by Saballah S. Khoury, B.A.G.A. Psy, *All Occasions Without a Teacher* (n.p., 1979).

The Baghdad Zoo (15)
Hans Blix is quoted by Patrick McLoughlin, 'Blix Says Iraq War Stimulated Terrorism' (Reuters, 13 October 2003).

Much of this poem was inspired by the efforts of Stephan Bognar of WildAid; see Hillary Mayell's 'Struggling to Save Baghdad Zoo Animals' <http://news.nationalgeographic.com/news/2003/06/0604 _030603_iraqzoo.html> (*National Geographic News*, 4 June 2003).

Hwy 1 (16)
The epigraph is quoted by Sinan Antoon, 'Of Bridges and Birds' <http://weekly.ahram.org.eg/2003/634/bo1.htm> (*Al-Ahram Weekly On-line*, 17–23 April 2003).

In the Leupold Scope (17)
Leupold Golden Ring Spotting Scopes, with a 12-40x60mm magnification, have long-range relief and very high resolution.

What Every Soldier Should Know (19)
The epigraph is from *The Social Contract*, translated by Maurice Cranston (Penguin Books, 1968).

English transliterations of Arabic words and phrases, in this poem, are from the Defense Language Institute Foreign Language Center (DLIFLC) handbook *Iraqi Basic Language Survival Guide* (February 2003).

Ashbah (28)
The title is Arabic for *ghosts*.

The quoted passage is from Fadhil al-Azzawi's poem 'Every Morning the War Gets Up from Sleep', translated by Salaam Yousif and al-Azzawi in *Iraqi Poetry Today: Modern Poetry in Translation*, No. 19, edited by Daniel Weissbort and Saadi S. Simawe (King's College London, 2003).

Trowel (33)
Halabjah is a city in Kurdish Northern Iraq which was attacked with chemical weapons by the Iraqi military under Saddam Hussein. There are reports of up to 5,000 killed in that attack alone.

The Martyrs Brigade (38)
The epigraph is from Abd al-Wahhab al-Bayyati's poem 'Shiraz Moon (section 11), translated by Farouk Abdel Wahab, Najat Rahman and Carolina Hotchandani, in *Iraqi Poetry Today: Modern Poetry in Translation*, No. 19, edited by Daniel Weissbort and Saadi S. Simawe (King's College London, 2003).

Dreams from the Malaria Pills (Barefoot) (42)
Ibn Khaldun (1332–1406) wrote the classic Islamic history of the world *The Muqaddimah, An Introduction to History*, translated by Franz Rosenthal (Princeton University Press, abridged edition 1967, 2005). Khaldun writes:

'In the *Ghayah* [The *Ghayat al-hakim*, ascribed to the famous tenth-century Spanish scientist Maslamah b. Ahmad al-Majriti] and other books by practitioners of magic, reference is made to words that should be mentioned on falling asleep so as to cause the dream vision to be about the things one desires. These words are called 'dream words'. In the *Ghayah*, Maslamah mentioned a dream word that he called 'the dream word of the perfect nature'. It consists of saying, upon falling asleep and after obtaining freedom of the inner senses and finding one's way clear (for supernatural perception), the following non-Arabic words: *tamaghis ba'dan yaswadda waghdas nawfana ghadis* [These magical words seem to be Aramaic.] The person should then mention what he wants, and the thing he asks for will be shown to him in his sleep' (p. 83).

Alhazen of Basra (48)
Abu Ali Hasan Ibn al-Haitham (965–1040 A.D.), known as *Alhazen* to the West, was an eminent physicist whose contributions to science remain vital and relevant to the present day.

Curfew (56)

The epigraph was said to me by an Iraqi translator who worked with my unit while in Mosul.

SECTION IV

The lines by Abdul 'Ala' A-Ma'arri are quoted by Sinan Antoon (see 'Hwy 1' above). This article features a passionate personal narrative of Antoon's native Baghdad. Of related interest: <http://www.soundvision.com/info/peace/baghdad.asp>.

Mihrab (58)

The title is Arabic for *gateway to Paradise*.

Milh (59)

The title is Arabic for *salt*.

Gilgamesh, in Fossil Relief (60)

The final line of this poem is from David Ferry's *Gilgamesh* (Farrar, Straus, and Giroux, 1992; Bloodaxe Books, 1993). Much of the information in the first stanza and the dedication is from William L. Moran's introduction to the same work cited above.

Sadiq (63)

The title is Arabic for friend.

The epigraph comes from *The Gulistan of Sa'di*, Chapter VIII, 'On Rules for Conduct in Life', Admonition 18 (written in 1258 A.C.E.). This can be viewed at: <http://classics.mit.edu/Sadi/gulistan.mb.txt>. The year this was written, Daras Salam (ancient Baghdad) was sacked – it is said that 800,000 lay dead in the streets after forty days of siege followed by forty days of brutal plunder.

Jameel (64)

The title is Arabic for *beautiful*.